The Wellbeing Guide

wellbeing escapes

First edition 2011
Second (revised) edition 2012
This third edition 2014

Published by Wellbeing Escapes Ltd
28–29 The Quadrant Business Centre
135 Salusbury Road, London, NW6 6RJ, UK

Written and edited by Miranda Vinall,
Stella Photi & Helen Greenhow

Designed by Marianna Tsikkos and Steven Randall
www.ocean-design.com

Printed by SS Media Ltd, UK

Text copyright © 2014 Wellbeing Escapes Ltd

ISBN 978-0-9570480-0-3

contents

welcome

Wellbeing Escapes specialise in providing their guests healthy holidays and experiences that will transform their lives. They are known as the UK's leading spa holiday and wellness experts.

The business was the brainchild of Stella Photi who founded the company out of a desire to make wellbeing more accessible to as many people as possible. As a working mother whose time was precious she found it impossible to find a service that would give her a wellness experience that she could trust would deliver when she really needed it.

Stella saw the need for a specialist that could provide a range of quality and authentic wellness experiences that could be pre-booked and pre-arranged to suit a variety of health and fitness needs. Stella wanted to create experiences that people could trust, knowing they had been carefully researched, involved genuine experts, offered great value, and, sometimes even life-changing results. She wanted to inspire people at all stages of their personal wellness journey – whether they were just starting, or were a well-seasoned wellness traveller.

Nearly a decade later and Wellbeing Escapes have become pioneers in the wellness travel world, crafting and creating a variety of innovative products for different needs and budgets but that all put the wellbeing of the guest at their very heart. Afterall, as Stella's motto goes, "everyone deserves a little wellbeing..."

guest testimonials

"Simply an amazing life changing experience...
I was sceptical at the start, but at the end
I felt calm, in control and happy."
Laura Barnes

"Exceptional 1-2-1 service. Amazing
experience... I will definitely be
recommending Wellbeing Escapes."
Asmah Bharti

"Efficient and easy to contact, the quality
of the information given was high... it felt
like they were there to help."
Sharifa Turner

"Very friendly, helpful & professional service.
Lovely people & I will definitely book
through Wellbeing in future."
Sharmen Smith

"I can safely say it was one of the best
holidays I have been on. Everything went
so smoothly from the flights, airport transfers
and the hotel itself."
Anne Coleman

A note from Stella

Hello and welcome to the third edition of our Wellbeing Escapes book!

From the very start Wellbeing Escapes has been about so much more than just providing spa holidays. I've always felt strongly that we should provide wellness experiences that give people a chance to take some time out from the daily grind, unwind, reconnect with themselves and focus on their health and wellbeing. This could be for a few days close to home or an extended period in an exotic location – whatever is right for you at that time.

Running a business, I know that sometimes it's hard to find time to take care of our bodies the way that they desperately need, especially after a long day hunched up over a desk. That is why Wellbeing Escapes strives to not only connect with our guests over their pursuit for a healthier, more balanced lifestyle, but also through an understanding of the challenges of busy daily lives. The aim has always been to play the part of a close friend who can cut through the jargon and make Wellbeing accessible and practical. We also have our fingers on the pulse of what's hot in the wellness world.

This book is a reflection of all we embody at Wellbeing Escapes. As well as including some wonderful articles from various holistic experts, life-coaches, fitness instructors, and meditation teachers who share our vision and passion for wellbeing, you'll also find my own personal tips for living a balanced life scattered around. Plus, if you're looking for some inspiration for your next escape then we also have a great selection from our portfolio at the back of the book.

Above all, we love hearing from our guests, sharing in their wellness journeys, and hearing what makes them tick. Don't forget you can always call us for a chat on 020 7644 6111; we're here to offer you an exceptional experience.

Wishing you health and happiness,

Stella Photi, Managing Director, Wellbeing Escapes

Our Vision & Values

We believe you should enjoy wellbeing experiences that leave you feeling healthier, refreshed and energised to bring positive change into your life.

We strive to make wellbeing easy and accessible; removing nonsensical jargon and creating a variety of options so you can find one that suits you and at the best value.

We've researched our destinations thoroughly to guarantee their authenticity so you can trust in the honest advice of our team, and the quality of your experience.

We believe your wellbeing experience should leave you feeling happy and informed so you can continue with your wellbeing journey when you return.

"The old kind of spa holidays where we lay in the sun all day seem to be definitely going out of style. This is where Wellbeing Escapes come in."

Lynne Franks, Holistic Lifestyle Guru

"Spa Holidays with a cultural kick — for great memories as well as a rested body and mind."

Psychologies Magazine

"Praise be for Wellbeing Escapes, a go-to for some of the world's greatest spas. The website offers a variety of retreats and packages for a much-needed mental detox."

Jessica Vince, Grazia

"Wellbeing Escapes is the John Lewis of healthy breaks – they gave me great advice, arranged everything seamlessly, and gave me a real deal!"

Ruby Wax, Comedian & Writer

"Take a mental detox. Give your mind the same attention as your body and book onto a Wellbeing Escapes Retreat."

Vogue UK Magazine

"The go to for super-spas."

The Sunday Times

wellbeing trends

Here at Wellbeing Escapes we've got our finger on the pulse as we're often advising resorts as to the trends in the market. And you can guarantee we shy away from the latest faddy diets, or gimmicky approaches.

More accessible, more affordable wellness

As people are more aware of preventative health they want new experiences that make them healthy and feel good. People are choosing to take more frequent short breaks to get an energising health kick. Our range of short Wellbeing Booster™ holidays are proving extremely popular. Getting away can bring a much needed change of scene, fresh air, healthy food, relaxation, fitness, and often the luxury of a few nights' decent sleep! It's also a more affordable and accessible wellness option for a lot of people to take shorter boosters over a long escape somewhere far flung.

Get connected

We are social animals and connection with others is an integral part of wellbeing. With the rising technology overload, the increase of single households and long hours at work, people, particularly in urban areas, are feeling more disconnected and sometimes lonely. When it comes to their wellness break they want to travel independently, but also come together with like-minded people. We now include more group activities like cooking classes, as well as shared dining tables to satisfy this growing need.

Fitness goes outdoors and experiential

There are so many ways to kick start fitness and discover the beauty of the local area that beat pounding the treadmill in the resort gym. Our Flexible Fitness™ packages pioneered this in our industry by giving guests a choice of daily fitness activities many of which are outdoors. Taking fitness holidays in the Alps is on the up. With magnificent mountains and big blue lakes, it's a joy to be out there in the open air. A study by the London School of Economics also found that people's happiness is greater in natural environments. Plus the altitude is really effective for boosting workouts so you get fitter in less time!

Healthy is the new thin

A real paradigm shift is happening. People are realising that looking good isn't about starving your body to achieve an impossible goal. More of us are realising that to look good, and we mean truly radiant, you have to be healthy. When your skin glows because it's getting all the right nutrients, it doesn't matter about the wrinkles – no one notices them when you're dazzling with health and happiness. To look good you ultimately have to feel good, and nothing makes you feel better than when you're in tip top health.

Bringing the mind onboard

From MPs doing it in parliament, high-powered executives citing it for their success in the City, and celebrities like Hugh Jackman tweeting 'It changed my life' – there's no denying it, meditation and mindfulness have hit the mainstream. Mindfulness is a fantastic tool that helps you get more out of your everyday life. From what you choose to eat, how you are at work, how you relax, more and more people are asking themselves if they are noticing what really fulfils them? Our Life-enhancement & Mindfulness Workshops have been a resounding success, with an astounding 100% of people who attended our day workshops saying they learned a new life-skill and would recommend the workshop to a friend. We expect this to be a trend with real staying power

Approaches

There are an infinite number of ways to stay happy and healthy, but we want you to pick the one that best suits you. In this section you'll find an in-depth guide to our favourite ways of getting fit and well. From how to lose weight and detox without damaging your body, to boosting your immune system – we take the mumbo jumbo out of complementary therapies and explain simply what each wellness approach is and how it can help you. We've also gleaned the wisdom of several world-renowned health experts to give us a deeper insight into how each approach works, and pestered them into sharing their top secret wellness tips.

"We must go beyond the constant clamour
of ego, beyond the tools of logic and
reason, to the still, calm place within us:
the realm of the soul."

Deepak Chopra

The different symptoms related to stress and how to combat them

Dr Andy Jones MD for Nuffield Health on how the body deals with stress

"More and more patients are visiting their GP with prolonged stress so it's a big concern for doctors. Regardless of why we are stressed the body always reacts in the same way: step one it produces more stress hormones; step two: immune function is inhibited, step three: the result may be a physiological symptom such as a stomach ulcer. Stress can reduce the white blood cell count opening the body up to infection and gastrointestinal issues.

In addition, many immune-related conditions and diseases that are associated with stress are characterised by the prolonged presence of proinflammatory cytokines which are small proteins released by cells in the body which cause inflammation. These illnesses include cardiovascular disease, osteoporosis, arthritis, type 2 diabetes, chronic obstructive pulmonary disease (COPD), other ageing-related diseases, and some cancers.

Regardless of activity levels acute or chronic stress can also result in back pain. The stress-related back pain diagnosis can be "psychosomatic" or "psycho-physiological". A psycho-physiological illness is any illness in which physical symptoms are considered the direct result of psychological or emotional factors. As for day-to-day wellbeing, a stressful day can lead us to seek dopamine as a reward and this means reaching for foods that are high in sugar or fats. Stress also produces cortisol, which has been found to directly influence appetite and cravings. The best advice any doctor can give to manage day-to-day stress is exercise regularly and eat healthily."

our top destinations for stress management

What are the different symptoms?
The symptoms of stress can present themselves in different ways. Physical, psychological and cognitive symptoms can all manifest when things get too much:

- **Physical symptoms** – headaches, asthma, stomach trouble, skin problems, obesity, high blood pressure, insomnia digestive difficulties and even strokes and heart attacks.

- **Psychological symptoms** – anxiety, depression, feeling overwhelmed, sheer fatigue, irritability and rumination.

- **Cognitive symptoms** – poor memory, lack of focus and disorganisation

"If you have a problem that can be fixed, then there is no use in worrying. If you have a problem that cannot be fixed, then there is no use in worrying."

Buddhist proverb

The good news is there are ways to beat the burnout

- **Get to know your limits and learn how to manage stress** – some people thrive on stress while others don't. Learn what makes you tick and when you feel as though your stress is getting too much then it's time for a pause.

  Take a short walk or go for a jog outdoors to clear your mind and remove yourself from any unwanted situations.

  Don't feel guilty about taking some time to yourself. Enjoy a spa treatment, or try aromatherapy oils like bergamot, chamomile, lavender, sandalwood or ylang ylang to relax you.

  Try meditation techniques – see our meditation section for simple and practical advice.

- **Pinpoint the causes of your stress** – Knowing that you're stressed won't provide a long-term solution. Figure out the reasons behind it and tackle them.

  Work – work smarter, not harder! Prioritise tasks and manage your time effectively so you're not spending all of your time at work, and avoid reading emails late at night.

  Too many commitments? Don't be afraid to wind down; sometimes we can stretch ourselves too much, so figure out which obligations you can sacrifice.

- **Eat healthily** – when you're stressed your blood sugar levels rise, but a healthy, balanced diet and eating regular meals can help to keep your blood sugar level steady.

- **Exercise regularly** – you don't have to train for a marathon, but regular gentle exercise will get your endorphins flowing which helps to reduce cortisol.

Stella's top tips

It's all too easy to let stress build up at work. Our breathing can get shallow which raises the carbon dioxide levels in our blood. This makes us feel anxious and stops our blood from being properly oxygenated. When you feel stressed at your desk turn away from your screen, shut your eyes and focus on the feel of your feet touching the ground. Breathe in and then out deeply for 60 seconds. With each breath feel the stress slowly lift from your body. This technique calms your muscles and lowers your cortisol levels.

stress-busting smoothie

When we're stressed we don't want to create something that takes too long to make! Blitz up these delicious ingredients to give yourself the necessary nutrients to help you cope.

Directions
1. Add all ingredients to your blender and blend until smooth, adding enough milk to your preferred thickness!

Why is this smoothie good for stress?

• Berries are one of the richest sources of immune boosting antioxidants which are shown to prevent free radicals in the body, and reduce inflammation, counteracting the effects of the stress hormone cortisol.

• Banana contains a wonderful amount of potassium which has been shown to lower blood pressure, preventing against heart disease and strokes.

• Aduna's Baobab is a magical super fruit powder. Just a few teaspoons can amp up the taste of the smoothie as well as the health benefits. It contains an abundance of vitamin C and malic acid, which has powerful energising properties, as well as helping to boost your immune system. Baobab also helps to promote a healthy nerve and digestive system and optimises iron intake, making you feel healthier, far more energetic and all together much happier!

Courtesy of Saskia Gregson-Williams at hipandhealthy.com

Ingredients

1 frozen banana

1/2 cup blueberries

Seeds of 1/2 a pomegranate

1 tbsp goji berries

1 tbsp ground flaxseeds

1/4–1/3 cup almond/oat/ brown rice milk

2 tsp Aduna's baobab powder

meditation

"It is not uncommon for people to spend their whole life waiting to start living."

Eckhart Tolle

Is meditation and mindfulness the new way of having it all?

Stuart Bold is the meditation and mindfulness expert for Wellbeing Escapes www.stuartbold.com

When I was asked to write an article around whether "meditation and mindfulness is the new way of having it all", I smiled at my own immediate answer. In my opinion the answer starts with an absolute, resounding and 100% "YES".

Yes, it is a way of 'having it all', if you look at the truly massive range of proven benefits, but it's certainly not a 'new' way. Meditation has been enhancing the lives of millions for thousands of years and mindfulness has always been part of this. It is however true to say that meditation and mindfulness are now very much 'of the moment' – and because of the many life skills they bring, they are now being sought by very many individuals, businesses and institutions around the world.

Why are meditation & mindfulness so highly valued right now by a new audience?

Partly it's because of the incredible range of the evidence-based benefits. In answering the question, yes, meditation & mindfulness is the way of having it 'all' – if you consider the following to constitute "all" – significantly better health & wellbeing (physical, emotional and mental); enhanced cognitive function and brain power; improved performance and success (professional and personal); greater happiness and fulfilment; better relationships and overall, a significantly enhanced quality of life.

These are just some of the proven benefits and health challenges addressed:

- Stress & anxiety reduction
- Deep relaxation
- Natural weight management
- Naturally reduce and 'reverse' ageing
- Blood pressure/cardiovascular health/atherosclerosis
- Stronger immune system
- Greater energy and vitality
- Insomnia/better sleep
- Improved mental health

"Meditation is empowering.
All you need is a little time each day."

- Reduced risk factors – heart disease, stroke & related conditions
- Pain management
- Management of long term conditions
- Diabetes
- Enhanced cognitive function –memory, concentration, focus, clarity, learning
- Migraines
- Enhanced management skills, greater communication and working relationship skills
- Emotional Intelligence
- Greater happiness

My approach when teaching/coaching – entirely secular (non-spiritual), evidence-based, practical, modern and focused exclusively on enhancing health, wellbeing, cognitive function, performance and happiness is another reason why so many people ask me to teach them meditation and mindfulness.

Additionally, once learnt, meditation is something you can access easily for the rest of your life, at any time you choose. It is empowering and all you need is a little time each day.

There is literally nothing else in the world that has so very many benefits and the evidence-base to back these benefits up.

My own work encompasses teaching meditation and mindfulness within the NHS, to GPs, in schools, for world leading spas, to private clients and high profile individuals, to world leading businesses and business leaders (up to CEO), to cancer patients and those with long term conditions, to armed forces veterans with PTSD and through to work with leading research institutions and Universities. I can honestly say that meditation and mindfulness will have a beneficial place In your own life and I invite you to give it a try – you will be pleasantly surprised!

our top destinations for meditation

Ananda, p62

Kamalaya, p72

SHA Wellness Clinic, p80

Shanti Maurice, p82

Spa Village Tembok, p84

SwaSwara, p86

Meditate don't medicate

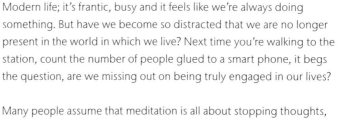

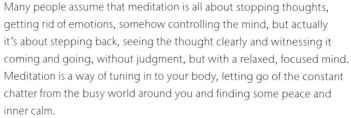

Modern life; it's frantic, busy and it feels like we're always doing something. But have we become so distracted that we are no longer present in the world in which we live? Next time you're walking to the station, count the number of people glued to a smart phone, it begs the question, are we missing out on being truly engaged in our lives?

Many people assume that meditation is all about stopping thoughts, getting rid of emotions, somehow controlling the mind, but actually it's about stepping back, seeing the thought clearly and witnessing it coming and going, without judgment, but with a relaxed, focused mind. Meditation is a way of tuning in to your body, letting go of the constant chatter from the busy world around you and finding some peace and inner calm.

As scientific research continues to gather evidence on the benefits of meditation, through neuroscience, psychology and neurobiology, it's heartening to see a growing movement to fund research in this area. Meditation is now even considered a serious form of treatment by the NHS and is regularly recommended as an effective tool for managing pain, depression, heart disease and diabetes.

Evidence-based Benefits of Meditation	
Combats stress	The root of many problems like depression, anxiety, insomnia, panic attacks, infertility and premature aging. By resting the mind the build up of stress and stagnant energy washes away leaving you clearer, alert, energetic and balanced.
Reduces biological ageing	By increasing DHEA (the 'youth hormone') levels. The Journal of Neuroscience published a paper stating that people who have regularly meditated for over 5 years or more have a biological age of 12–15 years younger than those who don't. A study done by Yale, Harvard, Massachusetts General Hospital has shown that meditation increases gray matter in specific regions of the brain and may slow the deterioration of the brain.
Boosts your mood	Meditation moves activity from right to left in the prefrontal cortex (behind the forehead). People who think more with the left part of the cortex are more positive, happy and relaxed rather than their right thinking counterparts.
Improves memory	The parts of the cortex associated with memory and decision making functions are thicker and therefore more effective in those who meditate.
Improves sleep	An 8 week study of insomniacs who were introduced to meditation resulted in 75% of those insomniacs being able to fall asleep within 20 minutes.
Reduces disease	A study of people with heart disease who were monitored over 5 years and used meditation as a relaxation technique found that 47% were less likely to suffer heart disease symptoms.
Helps PMS symptoms	A 5 month study of women who were introduced to daily meditation resulted in a 58% decrease in PMS symptoms.
Helps with addiction	Those with smoking, drinking and eating addictions are less likely to relapse if they regularly meditate. Just ask Russel Brand.

Stella's top tips

Am I too busy to meditate?
One of the hardest things people find is to sit still for 10 minutes. For those new to meditation, it can feel impossible but always remember to be gentle with yourself, take your time, try to relax and initially just go with the flow of your mind. It's not about obsessing over having a still mind, it's about letting thoughts come and go with total acceptance of the moment. Stick with it and carve out a bit of time each day and before you know it will become a regular habit.

meditation
Mindful eating

What did you have for breakfast? Be honest. Most people operate on autopilot, eating the same thing day in day and day out without even really noticing what's going in.

These days there are many social and environmental pressures that cloud our ability to listen to our body's needs. Mindfulness can help us. When you're being mindful you are tuning in to the present, and the moment, without giving it any judgement. Mindfulness becomes a tool to help you break free from bad eating habits, routines and even emotions that affect how or why you eat (or don't eat).

Our tips for eating mindfully

Truly taste each meal
Have you ever eaten an entire plate of food without actually tasting it? Try bringing all your senses to the table. Breathe in the aromas, notice the textures on your tongue, be aware of each bite from the moment it touches your lips to the moment you swallow.

Stop eating on the trot
When you're busy it's easy to scarf down a snack on the run. Try to avoid multitasking while you eat. Take a break so you can give it 100% of your attention, make food exciting again.

Are you really hungry?
Emotional eating can leave us munching away even when we aren't hungry. Gauge yourself on a scale of one to ten. Ask yourself each time you eat 'am I physically hungry?' Take cues from listening to your body and aim to eat until you are satisfied, so you're neither stuffed nor starving afterwards.

Observe your thoughts
Our relationship with food can be emotionally charged and tricky at times. When a critical thought creeps into your consciousness just remember that it is exactly that, a thought not a fact. Don't let negative thoughts sway your emotions or stop you from eating healthily.

Speak mindfully
People talk about fat and diets all the time but often without the awareness of what it might have on our self-esteem or the self-esteem of others. We've all been there chatting to friends or family about how we look e.g. the "I'm so fat; No you're not" debate but it will only serve to feed the critical thoughts in your own head, or affect others struggling with food issues.

fitness

"Junk food satisfies you for a minute,
being fit satisfies you for life."

Anonymous

Wellbeing Escapes 15 minute fitness routine by Graeme Marsh

Graeme Marsh is a Personal Trainer and Fitness Guru for Wellbeing Escapes

Sometimes it can feel as though there aren't enough hours in the day to commit fully to a proper exercise regime. But sometimes little and often can be just as effective and will more importantly keep you moving! Our fitness expert, Graeme Marsh gives us his 15 minute routine that can be done at home, in hotels, or even on the beach! No equipment is needed and it's a perfect way to warm up and stretch for the day ahead. Perform each set of exercises one after the other.

Exercise 1. Cats & Dogs
This exercise helps prepare the back for more active movement. I prefer not to perform this as a stretch but more as a mobility exercise, the simple difference being I don't advise forcing into the end of your range of movement. Try to flex and extend through the entire spine from the hips to the neck. 1 set of 10 flex/extends.

Exercise 1

"It isn't complicated. Move daily, eat clean, sleep better, laugh more often, and worry less, and you'll be well on your way to a healthier, happier life."

Exercise 2. Downward Dog

Part of the popular Sun Salutation routine, this yoga pose stretches out tight calves and hamstrings, helps extend the upper back, and strengthens the shoulders without being over strenuous. For those with very tight hamstrings, bend your knees to allow the chest to sink towards the floor and the hips to lift. Hold this pose for 5–10 deep breaths.

Exercise 3. Abdominal 100s

A great tummy toner. Tighten the stomach, lightly pressing the lower back against the floor. One at a time lift the legs up, the further the feet are from the hips the harder the exercise becomes. Make sure the tummy doesn't 'pop out' during this movement. Curl the top of the shoulder blades off the floor keeping the back of the neck lengthened. Maintaining normal breathing pump the arms for 100 reps.

Stella's top tips

Exercise outside rather than going to a gym. The fresh air helps to release endorphins giving you the positive vibes required to push yourself that little bit further. The varied scenery and surroundings also work wonders to take your mind off the physical exertion of your workout – another little trick to keep you exercising for longer.

Exercise 2

Exercise 3

Exercise 4. Warrior One

This classic yoga pose is a great hip opener, stretching the hip flexors, which all too often become shortened and tightened by hours spent at a desk or in a car. Step back from the standing position, keep the abdominals tight on this movement – don't let them pop out – and reach for the sky with both hands. Tuck the tailbone under to deepen the stretch on the front of the hips. You might well feel this in the front of your thigh too. Take 5 deep breaths on each side. Do an extra set if you feel particularly tight there.

Exercise 5. Glute Bridge

So often a poorly trained muscle group, effective glutes (the bum muscles) not only help protect the spine, but they look good too. Start with the double leg version and progress to a single leg version once you can do 20 slow speed repetitions without resting the bum on the floor. Keep the feet close to the hips, gently roll the hips back, squeeze your backside for all its worth and lift the hips to the ceiling, peeling the spine off the mat one piece at a time. Lower under control without losing the strong muscle contraction, brush the floor, and lift up again.

Exercise 6. Siff Squat

Finally, we finish off with a set of deep knee bends. Lift the arms in front and extend the upper back. Allow the knees to move forward over the toes but don't let them buckle inward. Lifting the heels challenges balance but also allows you to get a full range of motion on this movement. Don't bounce in this exercise, instead lower for a count of four and raise for a count of four. Do sets of ten reps at this speed and aim to add another repetition each time!

As with all types of exercise you know your body best. Work into movements slowly and progressively, and stop if any of them cause you pain or discomfort and seek advice from a medical professional.

Exercise 5

Exercise 6

our top destinations for fitness

fitness

Shake up your exercise regime

"Wow, I really regret that workout!" said no one, ever! Let's face it, no matter how tired you feel at the end, nothing is as satisfying as a good workout. However, sometimes it's hard to stay focused and motivated when your routine stays the same. The good news is that there are so many fitness classes out there to choose from which will help you to shake things up, the only problem is figuring out where to start.... We've put together some of our favourite classes and fitness methods to help you find what will work best.

Class & Description	Calories Burned	Pros	Cons
Kickboxing is a high intensity aerobic workout that uses every muscle in your body! It involves knee strikes, kicks and punches; punching bags and skipping ropes can be used as well.	700	• Burns lots of calories • Improves flexibility, muscle tone and strength • Learn self-defence • Varied and fun exercises • Improves your heart rate and lung capacity	• This is not for beginners; a basic fitness level is needed before starting otherwise you could injure yourself if your fitness level is too low or if it's not done correctly
Hatha Yoga focuses on strength, flexibility, posture and breathing to boost physical and mental wellbeing. The main components of yoga are postures and breathing.	200	• Helps with problems like high blood pressure, heart disease, aches and pains – including lower back pain, depression and stress • Increases flexibility and improves posture	• Not primarily a fat-burning exercise • If done incorrectly, you can injure yourself
Hot Yoga –Yoga for the hardcore. 90 minutes of abdominal-intensive, body-bending, fast-paced hatha yoga postures all carried out in 40 degree heat.	600	• Burns calories • Sweats out the toxins in your body • The heat helps to prevent injury, acting as a kind of safety guard but be careful all the same!	• Can cause dehydration if you don't drink enough water • Prepare to sweat... and sweat... and sweat – this is not a workout you can do on your lunch break
Pilates is a low intensity class based on the principles of rebalancing the body and bringing it into correct postural alignment.	280	• Provides whole body fitness • Strengthens without bulk • Increases flexibility and core strength • Increases energy • Gives you a longer, leaner appearance	• Low calorie burn, so not the most effective option if weight loss is your goal
Spinning is a moderate to high intensity indoor cycling workout where you ride to the rhythm of the music whilst the instructor calls out commands.	675	• Increases your cardiovascular fitness • Burns fat • Tones and shapes your legs, hips and bum • Increases leg strength and muscular endurance without building bulk	• Being in an enclosed space with lots of sweaty bodies isn't everyone's idea of fun • Classes can become monotonous
Zumba is a low to high intensity dance class with exotic rhythms and exercise moves set to high-energy Latin and international music.	600	• Exhilarating • Builds a sense of community between attendees • You won't be able to stop laughing • Good for all ages, sizes and abilities	• It can be difficult to learn some of the moves, but this can be part of the fun

gluten free power-up pancakes

These pancakes are not only delicious, they're vegan and gluten free banana pancakes and pack an incredibly energising, nutritious punch. Bananas are high in potassium and also help regulate your blood sugar, sustaining you through a workout. Coconut milk is highly nutritious and rich in fibre, vitamins and minerals.

Directions

1. Grind down the oats in a blender, grinder or food processor until it resembles flour. Set to one side.

2. Add the dates, and oat milk in the blender and blend until the date pieces have been obliterated into tiny fragments. Blend in the banana and all other ingredients until the mix is thick and smooth.

3. In a frying pan add a little coconut oil and spoon half a cup of mixture into the pan to make a small pancake. Don't be afraid if there is a lot of mixture on top. Cook on each side for roughly 2 minutes.

4. Meanwhile make the blueberry syrup. Really simple, add all the blueberries to a sauce pan with a tablespoon of water, let boil and pop until a syrup forms. Stir occasionally to make sure the bottom of the pan doesn't burn.

5. If you're making the coconut cream, just add the ingredients to a blender and blend until smooth. Drizzle on top. Add any extras and you're ready to enjoy!

Courtesy of Saskia Gregson-Williams at naturallysassy.co.uk

Ingredients

1 banana

1/3 cup brown rice flour

1 cup oats

1–1.5 cups oat/almond milk

2–3 medjool dates

1 cup blueberries

1 tbsp water

Coconut cream:

1/2 cup coconut milk (canned)

1 tbsp maple syrup

Extras:

Almond butter

Date syrup

weight management

"It is health that is real
wealth and not pieces
of gold and silver."
Mahatma Gandhi

Why is it difficult to lose weight? by Ian Marber

*Independent
nutrition therapist
and health writer
www.ianmarber.com*

Weight is a big deal. For many people what they weigh influences many areas of their life, not just what they choose to eat but what they wear and how they spend their leisure time. Many people spend years losing and gaining the same 5kg and it gets harder as time passes, meaning that we feel we have to try harder, cut calories that little bit more or run an extra half mile today. From a purely biochemical perspective losing weight is mostly quite basic. Reduce the energy that goes in and increase expenditure usually does it, but the methods we use and how we might feel during the process is hugely important, which is one reason why different eating methods work for different people.

Rather than think about weight, lets talk about money for a moment. We understand the basics about managing our finances and for the majority of us that means that we have a set amount each month to use to settle bills and look after our needs. If we spend a little too much we can borrow it in the form of an

overdraft, or use a credit card to manage larger purchases or for treats. We know that this money has to be paid back and as responsible adults, we factor those repayments into our budget. We also understand that the way we run our finances today will influence our credit record. A poor credit record makes getting a mortgage or even a mobile phone more difficult.

Now, think of losing and gaining weight in terms of credit and repayments. Trying to lose weight too quickly is the equivalent of borrowing money from payday lenders. Yes you will have the money in your account but the price you pay in the future is punitive. The same is true when we force weight loss through cutting those calories a little too much or exercising more than usual. You create an imbalance, which results in weight loss, but there is a price to pay. The metabolism responds by trying to hold on to stored fat next time around, as you have confirmed yet again, you haven't been managing your finances very well.

"Trying to lose weight too quickly is the equivalent of borrowing money from payday lenders."

It might be a slightly tortuous analogy, but you get the picture. With that in mind, here are some tips to help you balance the books.

1. Lose weight slowly

If a diet promises rapid results then you should consider it the equivalent of a get-rich-quick scheme, one that you would naturally cause suspicion. Lose weight slowly and steadily, no more than 1kg a week, a level at which shouldn't cause the human body to register any alarm and try to hold on to fat stores.

2. Combine the food groups

A mix of protein with complex carbohydrates (those that have plenty of fibre in them) together with lots of vegetables creates a meal or snack that delivers slow burn energy. In turn this reduces hunger making it easy to make smart food choices when its time to eat again.

3. Get active, but not too active

Whether you play tennis, run, go to the gym, enjoy football or dance classes, aim for regularity. Factor activity into your diary and keep it consistent as over-exercising, a common mistake when trying to lose weight, creates an imbalance that has to be corrected as soon as you ease off. If you can realistically manage three sessions of whatever it is then that's what you do – this week, next week, next month and so on.

4. What then?

As you aren't on a diet that has a beginning, middle and end, when you reach your target weight, you carry on. This is the way you eat now. If you 'come off the diet' or 'treat yourself, you deserve it' then you run the risk of the metabolism responding by being reluctant to let go of its stores.

5. But in real life….

Of course you will ease up, and you should, but weight needs managing just like your finances. Mostly responsible with some pleasure included.

Stella's top tips

Be accepting of your body. As you age your body changes, and it's important to accept that you'll never have the same body shape you had in your twenties, it's just a fact of life. The main thing is to stay healthy, active and put the right foods in your body. As the saying goes 'you'll never be as young as you are today' – so make the most of it!

Stop cellulite in its tracks

Cellulite – that dreaded word which evokes horror in even the skinniest of women – seems to be the one bodily imperfection that we just can't seem to shift. Those unsightly dimples with their orange peel effect make many women self-conscious about what they can wear and how much of their body they can put on show. However you feel about your cellulite, you can rest easy in the knowledge that just about every other woman has it (and some men too).

What is cellulite?

Despite its scary sounding name, cellulite is not a medical condition or a warning of a serious health problem; simply put, cellulite is nothing more than fat beneath your skin. It looks bumpy because the fat pushes against connective tissue, creating a dimpled effect on the skin above it. It isn't harmful, although most people aren't too fond of the way it looks. Weight isn't a factor either – you can still be skinny and still have cellulite.

The main causes are:

- **Genetics** – Your genes can make you more prone to cellulite with things like race, metabolism speed, fat distribution and circulation determining the likelihood of whether you'll be burdened with cellulite.

- **Hormones** – Many experts believe that oestrogen, insulin, noradrenalin, thyroid hormones, and prolactin assist in cellulite development.

- **Diet** – Including too much fat, salt, too many carbohydrates and not enough fibre in your diet means more cellulite.

- **Lifestyle** – Cellulite is more common in people who smoke, do little exercise, and sit down all day.

- **Clothing** – Tight elastic in underwear can restrict the blood flow and contribute to cellulite, so if ever there was an excuse for those infamous Bridget Jones knickers, this is it!

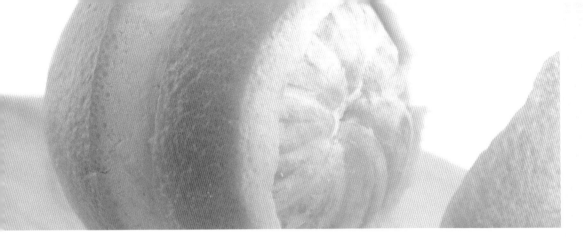

our top destinations for weight management

Ananda, p62

Absolute Sanctuary, p60

La Clairière, p76

Lefay Resort & Spa, p78

SHA Wellness Clinic, p80

Ti Sana, p90

How can we get rid of it?

OK, so some of those above causes can be out of our control, but the good news is that many experts agree cellulite can be reduced with a few changes. The fundamentals are exercise enough to burn off fat and boost circulation, eat the right foods and rid your body of all the harmful toxins which create cellulite.

Exercise – Forget products, creams and magic potions... exercise is one of the most effective ways to diminish dimples. Exercising for 30 minutes 5 times a week can burn calories as well as excess fat. This helps to reduce the lumps and bumps of cellulite whilst also keeping your metabolism elevated afterward. It will also serve to boost your blood circulation which flushes away fat and waste toxins from the skin's surface. Be sure to combine cardio exercises (running, cycling, swimming etc) with strength training (anything which builds muscles) to see the best results. Take a look at our 15 minute strength exercises on page 26.

Detoxify & eat correctly – Getting rid of the outward appearance of cellulite means addressing what's going on inside your body. To do this effectively detoxification and eating correctly go hand-in-hand: eating correctly will help to restore balance to your body and flush out any toxins and cleanse your body.

Make sure you get enough unprocessed and wholegrain foods and, where possible, eat foods raw – snack on fruit, vegetables and salad – and drink herbal teas and 1.5–2 litres of water a day to help cleanse your body of those cellulite-causing toxins. Avoid salt, sugar, processed foods, alcohol, caffeine and nicotine: these foods slow down your capacity to flush away toxins. Check out our section on detox for more ideas.

easy Japanese miso soup

Including miso soup in your diet may help you lose weight. Made from two fat-burning foods, seaweed and soya beans, this soup packs a powerful weight-loss and iodine-rich punch. Hokkaido University Graduate School of Fisheries Sciences in Japan found that eating a serving each day can increase your weight loss by 10 per cent.

Directions

1. Add water to a pan with the onion, carrot and celery, and cook for 20 minutes over a high heat. Then strain off the celery, onion and carrot so you just have the broth.

2. Add wakame seaweed to the broth and cook over high heat for another 5 minutes. Next add the tofu into cubes and cook for one more minute, and then remove the pan from heat.

3. Finally in a cup, dilute the miso paste with a little hot broth and then mix into the pan with the broth.

4. Serve with some chopped fresh chives.

Courtesy of SHA Wellness Clinic, Spain

Ingredients

1 litre of water

1 onion chopped in a half

1 carrot chopped in a half

1 branch of celery

2 shredded of wakame seaweed

3 tbsp of miso paste

1 green onion

100g of Tofu cut into 1 inch cubes

A pinch of salt

detox

"If you don't take care of this, the
most magnificent machine that
you will ever be given...where are
you going to live?"

Karyn Calabrese

Why detox is more important than ever by Elizabeth Montgomery

Elizabeth Montgomery is a London-based holistic nutritional therapist – holisticnutrition.co.uk

Given the current state of our planet detoxification is more important than ever for our health and wellbeing. Our bodies are constantly exposed to a wide spectrum of toxins that our ancestors never had to deal with: heavy metals, herbicides, pesticides, xeno-estrogens, radiation, fluoride. Incorrect food and drink choices, stress, lack of exercise, disconnection from nature, lack of sleep, negative thinking, all eventually lead to a state of 'dis-ease' which will manifest physically, mentally and emotionally in the body. Luckily with a little know-how it's easy to keep the detoxification functions of the body in check.

Love your liver

Liver health is essential when working on detoxification. It is the grand filter and essential detoxifier organ. The state of health of the liver will determine how efficiently it's able to release toxins out of the body. Signs of liver congestion include: headaches, skin disorders, nervous tension, anger, impatience and moodiness. In traditional Chinese medicine the flavour sour helps to target and open the liver detoxification pathways. Add in sour foods such as lemons, limes, raw sauerkraut and green apples in order to help the liver detoxify and maintain balance. Other key liver detox foods include onions and garlic, artichokes, olive oil and green vegetables.

Think green

Green foods also enhance the health of the liver. Vibrant green chlorophyll found in plants is almost identical in composition to human blood, and it is otherwise known as 'liquid sunshine'. Therefore, water-rich green leaves, green vegetables, wheatgrass juice and fresh green vegetable juices, are an integral part of any detox/health programme.

Eat superfoods

Add rejuvenating chlorella to your juices and smoothies. This ancient green algae repairs DNA and RNA within the cells along with

"Our bodies are constantly exposed to a wide spectrum of toxins that our ancestors never had to deal with."

removing heavy metals and carcinogenic compounds from the body. Mineral-rich seaweed is an amazing superfood and is very beneficial during these times of ever increasing exposure to radiation. It's great for the health of the thyroid gland – and it helps to remove radiation and heavy metals from the body. Sprouts are another incredible superfood with very potent medicinal properties. These are literally a powerhouse of nutrients that have between 20 to 30 times the nutritional value than the full grown vegetable. An easy tip is to add sunflower seed sprouts to your green juices for an added source of complete protein to stabilise blood sugar.

Sweat it out

Exercise is key when it comes to detoxification. It enhances circulation, lymph flow, cellular oxygenation, along with releasing numerous toxins through the sweat glands. Try power walking in nature, or short intensive interval training circuits, to fast track fat reduction and eliminate stored toxicity. Incorporate saunas into your detox programme, and seek out infra red saunas if possible, as they really target deeply embedded toxins in the cells of the body.

Elimination

Colon health is key when it comes to detoxification. When the colon is sluggish, food waste is reabsorbed through the bowel wall and back into the blood stream, which then perpetuates further toxicity and internal 'murky pond syndrome'. Increase the food transit time by including lots of fibrous vegetables. Add in colon cleansing support such as Aloe Vera juice and Psyllium seed husks for deeper cleansing.

Stella's top tips

Think about cutting out sugar. Too much sugar exhausts the adrenals and lowers immunity. In Chinese medicine it weakens the spleen and therefore dampness and heat are accumulated. Unnatural sugars particularly provide us with short bursts of energy which leave us feeling lethargic – try consuming less and watch how daily energy levels improve.

What does detox mean to you?

Think detox and most people's first thought is that it's something extreme, something that may involve starvation, fasting and deprivation. Even the word detox itself sounds harsh. But detoxing is simply a normal bodily function that your body is in fact really good at getting on with in order to eliminate the toxins that we come into contact with every day.

But here's the thing, even if you eat really healthily, there are times when your body becomes exposed to a higher than average amount of toxins. Maybe you live in a city where there are more pollutants, or you've been partying a little too hard, or you're under a lot of pressure a work – yes stress creates toxicity and acidity in the body.

Now more than ever, we are also exposed to toxins from the lotions we put on our skin every day, and use in our daily routines. Research by Bionsen, a natural deodorant company, found that before the average woman has even left the house in the morning she's exposed her body to a staggering 515 different synthetic chemicals from the shampoo, body wash, lotion, cosmetics and (worst of all) the perfume she uses. We don't help our bodies natural detox processes either by consuming sugary drinks, eating badly, or grabbing a liver congesting coffee on the way to work.

It's normal to feel like you want to 'detox' when you start feeling sluggish, unfocused or just generally run down. The truth is, even a healthy holiday will help boost your body's natural detox processes. Many of our guests call us asking for a detox holiday but in fact what they want is to eat healthily, exercise, de-stress and generally feel better. They want to find a balanced and integrated approach that can easily be implemented when back home to create a healthier lifestyle overall.

our top destinations for detox

Sometimes you may want or need to give your body a deeper cleanse for a particular health related reason. Even in these instances, the concept of detoxing has developed from the days of cutting out nearly every conceivable food type and having daily colonic hydrotherapy to a more holistic and integrated type of programme. Our detox programmes clear a path, so that your body can use its energies for regeneration and cleansing. Whether it's through Ayurveda, Naturopathy, or Fitness – whatever the detox approach you pick, the important element is that our guests are taught new tools to deal with the issues that they encounter in their day to day lives to keep those toxin levels from accumulating again.

This includes information on nutrition, mental relaxation, being aware and dealing with emotional triggers for certain addictions.

It is also worth expanding here on the importance of the emotional and mental aspect of a detox which is finally being recognised as equally if not more important than physical detoxification. It is widely accepted that mental stress brings on higher levels of cortisol that increase toxin levels. If, as part of a detox programme, we can find ways of helping our clients deal with the inevitable daily stresses that they will encounter when they go home then we at Wellbeing Escapes will have facilitated a good detox programme.

marinara zucchini fettucini

This easy raw food dish centres around zucchini (courgette) which is a total body cleanser. Plus it makes you feel like you're eating Italian without the heavy calories! Zucchini is abundant in nutrients and antioxidants, with the ability to cleanse the body of toxins and free radicals. It also cleanses the kidneys and blood vessels, preventing kidney diseases and excessive uric acid and lowers cholesterol levels.

Directions

1. Soak the sundried tomatoes in warm water for about 30 minutes until they are soft and pliable.

2. In the meantime, slice the zucchini in thin pieces. Add salt and mix all the slices together.

3. When the sun-dried tomatoes are ready, blend them with the fresh tomatoes, onion and garlic until it makes a smooth marinara sauce.

4. Place zucchini on the plate and add the marinara sauce on top. Dress with dice-shaped tomatoes and a dash of pesto sauce. Garnish with fresh basil.

Serves 1

Courtesy of Absolute Sanctuary, Thailand

Ingredients

250g zucchini

50g sun-dried tomatoes

100g fresh tomatoes

A pinch of sea salt or Himalayan salt

2–3 fresh basil leaves

Half an onion

1 garlic clove

"You can't help getting older, but you don't have to get old."

George Burns

How to slow the ageing process by Dr Simone Laubscher

Dr Simone Laubscher, nutritional doctor from Rejuv on Harley Street www.rejuv.co.uk

Alkalize – The key to good health and slow ageing is to get your pH right. All this means is you need to eat more alkaline foods and less acidic foods. Follow a basic rule of 80% plants and 20% animal products and junk foods. Enjoy your life and use the 80:20 rule so most of the time you make healthy choices and 20% of the time you have fun.

Spice up your life – Your immune system loves herbs and spices such as turmeric, cayenne, pepper, chilli, garlic, ginger, basil, coriander and lemon grass. Since 70% of your immune system is in your gut, what you eat creates the foundation to your health. A good way to kick start your day is with warm or room temperature water with lemon, ginger and 1 pinch of cayenne pepper!

Hydrate – Since the average human body is made up of 70 trillion cells and 60% of your body is made up of water, then your body needs good clean water, about 2 litres per day.

Go easy on the caffeine. If your water to caffeine intake is correct with 8 glasses of water to 1 caffeinated drink per day then your cells will look like big fat grapes instead of shrivelled up raisins! This will allow goodness into the cell and toxins out. This is the key to looking and feeling amazing – like you on a good day, every day!

Stay lean – Toxins live in our body fat so if we want to look and feel youthful and prevent disease, then we need to stay healthy and lean. Try adding what I call a 'Rejuv Detox Day' to you week where you eat vegan for the day and drink 1–2 veggie juices. Mondays are good so you pay for some of the fun you had over the weekend.

Moisturize from the inside out – For your skin to stay youthful you need to make sure you are getting enough essential fatty acids and omega 3 in your diet. This way your hair, skin, nails and joints will stay youthful

longer. With a lot of the world being toxic these days supplement with a vegetarian form of omega 3 in the form of flaxseed oil or milled flaxseeds for a safe bet.

Keep your pipes moving – For your body to detox effectively each day and for you to stay youthful you need to be able to go to the loo each day and not skip a day or two. Taking in enough fibre (and water) is the key. If you want to stay lean and don't want to carb load then why not use psyllium husks or milled flaxseeds instead. These two products will swell in your digestive system making you feel full but also act like a pipe cleaner throughout your intestines and colon taking all the toxins with it. Staying regular is a key to staying youthful!

Chew – I know it sounds silly but so many people inhale their food and don't chew anymore! It takes 20 minutes for the brain and stomach to connect so if you eat too

quickly the brain and stomach don't have time to connect and you end up over-eating. This will not only lead to weight gain but put too much pressure on the digestive and metabolic systems. The goal is to chew each mouthful at least 20 times.

Oxygenate – One of the best ways to do this is through laughter. Lift your spirits and hang out with friends who make you laugh and/or watch funny films. Also breathing on purpose is key so that you exhale as much of the CO_2 out of the body as possible. Each day try to breathe deeply 5–10 times and then exhale as much of the air possible to remove all the stale air in our lungs. This will have a knock on effect right down to you cells and boost your immune system. So shake off your troubles, develop a positive mindset with a light hearted take on life and oxygenate!

Stella's top tips

I love face oils and rosehip oil is my miracle worker. Contrary to popular belief, face oils are not just for people with dry skin but work just as well on those of us who have combination skin. When applying the oil you can give yourself a one minute face massage which stimulates cells. I apply my oil at night instead of a night cream and also a few drops in the morning under my moisturiser. Trust me, it doesn't leave you with an oily film, rather super-soft skin. There are many face oils on the market but my current favourite is the organic rosehip oil by trilogy. It's packed with antioxidants so it's great for keeping my skin looking young and supple.

Five foodie favourites for healthy skin

Eating the right foods can give you a smoother complexion, thicker hair, and stronger nails, often more so than when you were younger and eating all the wrong things. Wrinkles will happen to us all, but if your skin is glowing with health and vitality then honestly no one will really notice them anyway.

1. Make sure your diet contains plenty of antioxidants (which help slow down cellular ageing). Fresh fruits and vegetables are the best sources of natural plant antioxidants. Try drinking a green juice with a variety of veg once a week. Veg is rich in chlorophyll which helps to purify the blood, build red blood cells, detoxify the body and give you an energy hit. Try a carrot, a cucumber, 4 celery stalks, a fennel stalk, some spinach leaves and a piece of ginger juiced up together. Then start experimenting – just think fresh, organic and colourful.

2. Food combine. By eating protein and carbohydrates at separate meals, you'll prevent unnecessary fermentation in the colon and increase nutrient absorption into the blood. You can eat salads, non-starchy vegetables, roots, seeds and herbs with either protein or carbs at the same meal.

3. Always eat fruit on its own, at least 30 minutes before or after eating something else. It's digested by the body extremely quickly and it's best eaten on an empty stomach, preferably in the morning with no other foods. If you eat fruit after a meal it gets stuck behind the other food that takes longer to digest so will just sit and ferment in the gut. Melon is the fastest of all fruits to digest so either eat it alone or leave it alone!

4. Include lots of fibre in your diet. It keeps your intestinal tract regular, and enhances your elimination of waste products from your body. Some people with skin problems suffer from constipation because they fail to feed themselves with good sources of fibre. Whole grains, green vegetables and sprouted seeds are all excellent sources.

5. Make a honey facemask. Externally apply organic, raw honey to your skin once or twice a week and leave on for about 30 minutes then rinse off with warm water. It's an amazingly simple trick which leaves skin soft, nourished, supple and young as honey contains potent antibacterial, antioxidant, antiseptic and moisturising properties.

our top destinations for healthy ageing

Chiva-Som, p66

Fusion Maia, p68

Kamalaya, p72

Kempinski Gozo, p74

Lefay Resort & Spa, p78

Spa Village Tembok, p84

garden salad with wasabi dressing

Full of nutrient rich, powerful ingredients such as goji berries, avocado and grounded flax seeds, this is a powerful anti-ageing salad. Goji berries are traditionally regarded as one of the most nutrient dense and important medicinal herbs in China as they have many medicinal benefits, resulting in a strengthened immune system function and extra protection for the liver cells. Due to its high antioxidant activity, goji berries are believed to slow down the aging process. Try the wasabi dressing, it's just delightful!

Directions

1. Prepare the dressing by placing all ingredients, except olive oil, into a blender. Blend on medium setting for about 30 seconds. Switch to the lowest setting, and very slowly pour the olive oil into the blender. It is important that the oil is added slowly, otherwise the dressing will separate.

2. Now, prepare the salad. Tear the baby cos, green oak and red oak leaves into bite sized pieces. Leave the rocket leaves whole. Place all the salad leaves in a large salad bowl and toss lightly.

3. Sprinkle the salad leaf mix with the rose apple, avocado, beetroot, seeds and goji berries. Lightly 'lift' the salad with your fingers to distribute the ingredients.

4. Drizzle with salad dressing just before serving.

Serves 2

Courtesy of Kamalaya Wellness Sanctuary, Koh Samui

Ingredients

Salad:

500g baby cos
(romaine lettuce)

40g green oak leaves

300ml red oak leaves

10ml rocket leaves

30g rose apple, cubed

30ml avocado, cubed

30ml beetroot, cooked,
peeled & cubed

500g pumpkin seeds

40g sunflower seeds

10ml flax seed, ground

30g goji berries

Wasabi dressing:

100ml coconut water

50ml apple cider vinegar

50ml virgin olive oil

5g wasabi powder

20ml lime juice

60g coconut meat

know before you go

At Wellbeing Escapes, we really do want you to get the most out of your holiday and to return not just rested and relaxed, but glowing and full of new intentions. We know that the weeks and days leading up to a holiday are often stressful, as you try to get everything done before you leave. Try not to push yourself too hard, you will only be away for a few weeks and the world will still be there when you return. To help you cope with pre-holiday stress, here are a few of our hopefully helpful hints.

Lists

We are avid list-makers – which is ideal when you need a reminder for all the things you want to do before leaving home. It should include everything from buying new knickers to handing over documents at work to the telephone number of the kennel where your dog will be staying. We find that once committed to paper or a smart phone, it's easier on the brain. Also list everything you need to take away, from passport to perfume.

Home sweet home

Definitely don't try and leave your home spotless before you go on your spa holiday. Yes, it's nice to come back to a clean place, but it doesn't need to look like a show home. Your home will only gather dust while you're gone. Ditto with the laundry, just prepare the clothes you want to take with you. Save any ironing for when you're away – it crumples in the suitcase anyway.

Prepare your body

Easing your body into a new routing is particularly important if you're heading for a detox or weight management break. Aim for an early start on what's ahead of you by cutting back on caffeine and having your final evening meal at home before 7pm, making sure it's low in carbs. This allows your digestive system time to work before bedtime, resulting in better quality of sleep. It also helps those who push themselves with an extra workload before departing. You risk arriving exhausted and wasting the first few days of their holiday having to just sleep to recover.

Protect & soothe

The answer to most things is water. Drink lots of it, especially when you're travelling or tired, to keep you hydrated. If you're heading off anywhere near mosquito territory, prepare in advance by taking Vitamin B complex supplements a month before you depart. Mozzies hate whatever smell the vitamins emit. Also avoid eating foods high in potassium (such as bananas) as this attracts them. Be sure to take some essential oils; lemongrass and citronella are good repellents, lavender will not only help take away the sting and any itching but will also help you sleep, while tea tree oil is good for bites, cuts and acts as an all-round antiseptic.

Pack light

It's quite usual to be provided with 'spa wear' at Destination Spas for you to lounge around in, wear to holistic classes or take to the spa. These garments are comfortable and practical, such as Indian Kurta Pyjamas or Thai Fisherman Pants, with fresh sets provided each day. This means you don't have the stress of what to wear, you can blend in with your fellow guests, avoid getting your own clothes stained with massage oil, and best of all, you can travel light, packing only the essentials.

Jet lag

Our suggestion is to try and slot into the time frame of your destination as soon as you step on the plane, so if that means you should sleep, then try and do so. This will really help kick-start the adjustment. Make sure you continue to drink lots of water and try and get some sun on the back of your knees when you arrive.

Suncare & aftercare

Our mantra? Always treat the sun with care and reverence. Avoid being in the full glare of a midday sun, always wear sun protection lotions, try to keep your face out of the sun, wear a hat and don't miss the knobbly bits, like ankles, knees and toes, which are often forgotten in the great slathering process. But if you do, Pure Aloe Vera gel is excellent for soothing sunburn.

post spa support

We know how it is when you arrive fresh from the spa, sun kissed skin and baggage left behind, there's a spring in your step and you're ready to take on the world. But we also know about that niggling voice that doubts your progress and asks 'how do can I possibly keep up with all of these changes once I'm back in the real world?' Well we've got a few trouble-free tips to keep you on the straight and narrow once you're back to the land of rain and routine...

- Keep a journal or progress diary. It's a really great way of keeping track of your health whilst regimenting your lifestyle at home. Your journal needn't be restricted to scribbling on a notepad either, exercise your creative flair using photos and artwork to add a bit of colour as you manage the new you.

- Instead of guzzling down an espresso and suffering the dreaded mid-morning crash try hot water with a hint of lemon. Its helps flush away any bodily toxins, boosts your immune system and gives a caffeine free kick of natural sugars to start your day.

- Be sure to take regular meals, it keeps your metabolism active and can quash the temptation to snack. But if temptation proves too much keep a bag of seeds in your desk drawer, it's a great healthy alternative to salty snacks and cakey treats.

- Try to cut back on unnaturally occurring sugars altogether. Whilst a bar of dairy milk or a French fancy might give us the sensation of wellbeing they leave us with cravings, a widening waistline and diminished returns. Instead find your fix in fresh fruit, it's packed with goodness and has that same sense of sugary satisfaction.

- Be sure to snuggle up with at least one lie in a week. Catching up on those lost hours of rest gives our bodies time to recover and heal from the stress of the working week. Trouble sleeping? Try drinking a glass of cherry juice each day, studies show it can replenish melatonin levels which help regulate the sleep cycle and can reward us with up to an extra hour of deep sleep per night.

- Take a time out each day. It's easy to get caught up in the hustle and bustle of the everyday and forget to stop and think about our wellbeing. Leaving our work area and concentrating on our sensory awareness for ten minutes each day will have a grounding effect and increase positive energies. Take a moment to be aware of sounds, sights, tastes and smells, breathe in slowly and find peace within yourself, it's the secret to keeping that spring in your step.

Destinations

We've hand-picked some of the most prestigious wellness resorts in the world, where you can experience a first-class healthy holiday. We work hard to deliver exclusive offers and packages at each destination so that you get the most benefit from your holiday. You may have noticed a little symbol next to each wellness approach in the previous section. This key lets you know if the spa centre offers the wellness approach you're looking for, so you can flip to it easily to find out more about the destination itself. Don't forget we offer more destinations on our website. Feel free to visit our home page or call us for a chat; we love talking to you!

 Detox

 Yoga & Pilates

 Weight Management

 Meditation

 Fitness

 Holistic Healing

 Stress Management

 Wellness Waters

 Healthy Ageing

 Destination Spa

 Ayurveda

Absolute Sanctuary

With a homely atmosphere, this Moroccan-inspired boutique property in Thailand is ideal for nurturing yoga bunnies and detox devotees. Nourished by fresh juices, food from the Love Kitchen, and all the yoga you can handle, it's ideal for those seeking a complete health overhaul.

Wellness Approach

A comprehensive holistic approach to health means Absolute Sanctuary can deliver truly transforming results and long-lasting benefits for guests. Yoga is their main area of expertise, though the team of qualified naturopaths, nutritionists and holistic healers have developed an impressive detox and rejuvenation programme.

Food

How could you not adore a place where the main restaurant is called The Love Kitchen? It's where the most nurturing of foods is prepared and cooked with loving care. Better still it's delicious whether you are on a detox diet or weight management programme, while the menu also caters for vegetarian as well as non-vegetarian aficionados. The ingredients are wherever possible local, natural, organic and of course, fresh be they from land or sea. All the various dishes are light, clean-tasting and healthy, while at the same time catering for guests individual tastes and needs.

Fitness & Activities

Offering boutique health and wellness programmes, Absolute Sanctuary specialise in detox, yoga, and now excitingly new Reformer Pilates sessions. There is also a stunning infinity-edge swimming pool, large sun lounge area, Pool-side juice bar, spa centre boasting a fabulous selection of treatments, infra-red sauna, steam room, free Wi-Fi access and a free shuttle service to the nearby beaches if you fancy a dip. Plus, with three yoga studios, there is plenty of space for all these classes or to practice on your own.

We Love

The wide variety of yoga styles — Hatha, Restorative, Hot, Yin, Vinyasa Flow plus their own Absolute Fit. The different class levels means there is something for everyone, from beginners to challenging classes.

Location
Koh Samui, Thailand

Rooms
38

Freestyle Spa Facilities
Steam Room

Ananda in The Himalayas

In one of the most beautiful locations on earth. Nestled in the foothills of the Himalayas and overlooking the valley of the sacred River Ganges, sits this world-class health resort created around a Maharajah's summer palace and gardens. Expert health guidance is provided by a team who are as au fait with modern techniques as they are with ancient Indian traditions.

Wellness Approach

The Ananda Wellness Centre offers each guest a consultation with an expert doctor to determine a personalised Ayurvedic programme, which includes spa treatments, cuisine, yoga and meditation. A favourite of British royalty, the focus here is the Ayurvedic traditional holistic practice of balancing mind, body and spirit. There's a gym and heated outdoor swimming pool, while yoga and meditation can be practised outdoors. Their extensive spa menu has over 79 different treatments, plus there's a programme of lectures, as well as visiting Masters, throughout the year.

Food

After a wellness consultation to discover your Ayurvedic body type known as your dosha, your food will be customised to suit your dosha, to optimise health and achieve balance. Don't expect just Indian flavours, the choices are Western as well as Asian, to maximise variety plus there's a sociable sharing table at dinner for those travelling alone.

Fitness & Activities

The daily group activities focus on the ancient disciplines of yoga and meditation but also include other activities such as fitness classes, nature walks and weekly Ayurvedic cooking classes. Experience aqua yoga, join lectures that explain the science of Ayurveda, sample a golfing skills workshop; there are enough free daily activities to enjoy a true wellness experience. Have a game on the 9-hole golf course or in the billiards room, or join a trip to a local temple, trek local beauty spots, take a wildlife safari or follow in the footsteps of the Beatles and visit the pilgrim town of Rishikesh.

Location
Himalayas, near Rishikesh, India

Rooms
75

Freestyle Spa Facilities
Comprehensive hydrotherapy facilities, including a steam room, sauna, whirlpool, Kniepp foot bath and a cold plunge pool.

Aphrodite Hills Resort Hotel

The Greek goddess of love, Aphrodite, was believed to have emerged from the sparkling stretch of Mediterranean Sea, right in front of the site on which the luxurious Aphrodite Hills resort is built. Today the island combines a history steeped in myth and legend, with Greco-Roman architecture, stunning natural beauty, and classic Cypriot hospitality.

Wellness Approach

Aptly named 'The Retreat', this impressive award-winning spa has a huge range of treatments for pampering, relaxation and light detox. A for adults-only spa facilities and an expert team of therapists await guests, as well as bespoke treatments and sublime rituals from ESPA, a world renowned brand offering effective, natural and results driven products and treatments.

Food

Ingredients from local markets prepared by the chefs at Aphrodite Hills promise a feast for the senses. There are several restaurants offering Mediterranean and international cuisine, and a pool bistro, plus a cluster of restaurants and cafés to choose from in the village square, from Indian, to Cypriot and Italian. Within the resort, Eleonas offers an a la carte menu, and a buffet, the Leander offers an Asian menu, the Mesogios, which is Greek for Mediterranean, uses local cooking

methods to create fresh and healthy food, and the Ifestos is an casual style brasserie.

Fitness & Activities

Whether it's swinging round the championship standard 18-hole golf course, or playing tennis with professional instructors, Aphrodite Hills does not do fitness by halves. With four floodlit hard courts, the Aphrodite Hills' tennis centre boasts fabulous views over the coast and The Tennis Academy is the best in Cyprus. Aside from competitive sports, the woodland stables offer horse-riding for exploring the mountainside through undiscovered paths behind the resort. For sun seekers, The Cove beach and Zias Beach club are all within a 15 minute complimentary shuttle bus transfer from the resort.

Location
Near Paphos, Cyprus

Rooms
290

Freestyle Spa Facilities
Separate male and female saunas, infinity pool, relaxation area and whirlpool.

Chiva-Som

Chiva-Som is one of the best and most established health resorts in the world. Located in the Thai royal town of Hua Hin, within tropical gardens, it has a very comfortable climate. Don't be put off by the touristy bars of Hua Hin, as Chiva-Som is a haven of peace and serenity.

Wellness Approach

This is a place where you can embark on your own personal wellness journey, supported and guided by a team of highly qualified experts who will help you achieve your goals. Even though celebrities often visit, don't expect showy glitz and glamour – the resort is welcoming yet serious about making sure you leave healthier than when you arrived. There are an extensive range of holistic treatments on offer – from naturopaths, homeopaths, Traditional Chinese Medicine to even colonic hydrotherapy for the dedicated!

Food

Fantastic award-winning spa cuisine with fat, calorie and carbohydrate counts showing on all menus and buffets. Detoxifying, with minimal salt, and using organic produce from the Chiva-Som gardens, the food is as delicious as it is good for you. The secret lies in the creative approach of Chiva-Som's Master Chef, who cleverly combines Thai and Western cuisine.

If you're travelling solo and feeling sociable, you can join the friendly sharing table.

Fitness & Activities

On arrival, there's a personal health and wellness consultation with a natural health practitioner, to determine the best treatments and activities to achieve your desired goal. The options range from aqua-aerobics, water sports, gym work-outs, Pilates and beach activities, to the time-honoured Eastern techniques of yoga, Tai-Chi and Thai boxing. An alternative path is the holistic approach; Chiva-Som provides a comprehensive choice of therapies. Meditation, stress management, mind-training and other programs unique to Chiva-Som, can help you to reach the perfect balance of mind and body.

We Love

There's so much to love about this top-notch Destination Spa that it's hard to pick! However, the ratio of four staff for every guest is superb as you feel supremely well looked after at this luxurious bolt-hole.

Location
Hua Hin, Thailand

Rooms
58

Freestyle Spa Facilities
Separate male and female Water Therapy Suites with sauna, steam room, jacuzzi and plunge pools, heated waterbeds for relaxation, and bathing pavilion with indoor heated lap pool, unisex steam room, plunge pool and relaxation area.

Fusion Maia Da Nang

Fusion Maia, with its beach-front setting, nearby cultural heritage and bespoke tailoring shops, not to mention at least three inclusive spa treatments each day, is a treat for the senses! On top of this healthy indulgence, local excursions to traditional Hoi An or rural paddy fields will offer an insight into the warmth of Vietnam.

Wellness Approach

Boasting the largest spa in Vietnam with 50 therapists, the Maia Spa really is the jewel in the resort's crown. Apart from the indulgence of unlimited inclusive spa treatments, the spa's philosophy of Natural Living Practices is a seven-principle guideline on how to achieve a balanced lifestyle. From the massage oil to the food served in the restaurant, they all revolve around a different theme each day, to stimulate your senses to facilitate mental, emotional and physical wellbeing.

Food

Fusion food does exactly that, fusing light and fresh Vietnamese ingredients into healthy and delicious dishes. From spring rolls to salads, wraps to raviolis, everything is cooked to be refreshing and tasty, without a deep-fryer in sight. The resort also offers breakfast 'anytime, anyplace' which gives you the luxury of time to have breakfast whenever and wherever you choose, so there's no need to set an alarm...

Fitness & Activities

When you're not luxuriating in the spa, perhaps take part in spa workshops where you can learn to craft your own homemade remedies, or join daily fitness classes like Pilates and yoga. If you're curious about the local region and customs, your own Fusionista Host will be happy to chat about real life in Vietnam. Or hop on one of the resort's four free daily shuttle buses and explore nearby Hoi An! Fusion Maia also offers group excursions to local markets and a local orphanage which is supported by the resort, so you can really experience the essence of the culture.

We Love

When it's a full moon, the quaint nearby town of Hoi An turns off all their electric lights so only the light of the moon and candle-lit lanterns abound. The resort organises a shuttle bus to take guests there to witness this truly beautiful event.

Location
Hoi An, Da Nang, Vietnam

Rooms
87

Freestyle Spa Facilities
16 treatment rooms, beauty salons, whirlpools, steam rooms, saunas, yoga studio, spa workshop area and spa library.

Gleneagles

From the moment the kilt-clad concierge open the grand oak doors you'll feel at one with the beating heart of Scotland. Once described as the 'Riviera in the Highlands', this impressive country pile has acres of land, a serious spa and several excellent restaurants. It's hard to imagine ever wanting to leave.

Wellness Approach

Gleneagles philosophy is bliss-inducing wellness in a luxurious setting. As one of the only two ESPA spas operating in the UK, it offers Traditional Chinese Medicine, Ayurvedic massages plus a plethora of beauty treatments and facials. With its modern design and state of the art technology, this spa goes beyond the luxurious to the sublime.

Food

From the Full Scottish Breakfast to the two Michelin-star restaurant of Andrew Fairlie, whatever tickles your taste buds, Gleneagles can deliver. Meat lovers can enjoy locally sourced, pure pedigree Scotch beef (you can even cut your own steak!) and whether your dietary focus is maximum indulgence or moderation, dining at Gleneagles promises to be a delight to the senses. The only problem foodies face is deciding between the tempting aromas of Scottish, French or Mediterranean cuisine, and choosing from the unrivalled list of fine wines and whiskey.

Fitness & Activities

On a massive estate boasting three golf courses, including the PGA Centenary Course designed by Jack Nicklaus to host the 2014 Ryder Cup, Gleneagles really is a golfer's paradise. But if you don't fancy teeing off there are plenty of scenic footpaths, clay-pigeon shooting and dog-handling schools and even a rugged off road 4x4 track. There's also a wide range of complimentary, daily fitness classes available including Zumba, Pilates, Aquafit, Spinning, Yoga, Tai Chi and Body Pump. We just dare you to be bored.

We Love

Getting outdoors and active in the majestic rolling hills of Perthshire. From horseriding to golf to cycling; with such extensive grounds come any number of outdoor opportunities.

Location
Perthshire, Scotland

Rooms
232

Freestyle Spa Facilities
Indoor and outdoor swimming pools, tennis courts, state of the art gym, vitality pool, tropical showers, ice fountains, saunas, and crystal steam rooms.

Kamalaya Wellness Sanctuary

Kamalaya was created around a Monks' Cave, and the accumulated energy from centuries of prayer and meditation lends the resort a powerful meditative magic. Built into the hillside, the rooms and villas are almost hidden in the landscape, while the yoga pavilion looks over treetops down to the resort's own private beach.

Wellness Approach

Nowhere does a detox quite like Kamalaya. Starving your body is not the key to health, so detoxes are instead fully supervised, deeply nourishing affairs that strengthen your cellular structure and release accumulated toxins, boosting immunity and overall energy levels. So this extensive holistic and complementary approach is why 'Wellness Sanctuary' is the perfect description for Kamalaya. Holistic medical experts are impressive – naturopaths, homeopaths, traditional Chinese Medicine doctors, nutritionists and a conventional medical doctor, are all on call for diagnostic testing, food intolerances and body imbalances. It's not all serious though; holistic massages, facials and body wraps are available too.

Food

Nutrient-rich food is integral to Kamalaya's wellness philosophy with an emphasis on high quality, fresh ingredients and organic wherever possible. Kamalaya's healthy cuisine is inspired by a fusion of Eastern and Western traditions. Menus include vegetarian options, as well as seafood, poultry and lamb dishes. If you want to detox, fresh juices, signature tonics and herbal teas are available with specially prepared meals to meet your dietary requirements.

Fitness & Activities

Kamalaya is the perfect place for yoga. Practise at the semi-outdoor hilltop Yoga Pavilion and the open Yoga Sala or the enclosed Yantra Hall. Pilates and Tai Chi are also popular. As well as an extensive wellness and treatment area, plunge pools, a steam cavern, sauna and gym are provided for your wellbeing. Just a ten minute drive away, you can go elephant trekking and meet some very cheeky monkeys.

We Love

The different levels of detox. A holiday at Kamalaya is ideal for those who are new to detox while also appealing to those who want to address more serious health or weight concerns. Make your choice and an individual programme will be tailored for you – otherwise simply relax, enjoy and come home feeling fitter and healthier.

Location
Koh Samui, Thailand

Rooms
34 rooms & 25 villas plus an additional 15 new suites from early 2015

Freestyle Spa Facilities
Herbal steam cavern with its own waterfall, three plunge pools all at different temperatures, plus plenty of quiet relaxation areas.

Kempinski Hotel San Lawrenz

Located on the sleepy island of Gozo, Malta's little sister island, the resort has a dramatic location, looking out over rugged terrain covered in lush vegetation. Quiet and peaceful, the island has bags of local charm. The people are friendly and the churches pretty, making it a great basis for a relaxing and cultural retreat.

Wellness Approach

Recognised as one of the best and most authentic Ayurveda spas in Europe, guests on an Ayurvedic programme are seen by a doctor and prescribed a personalised plan which involves treatments performed by staff trained in Kerala (the birthplace of Ayurveda). Tailored diets, herbals remedies and yoga complete the experience. Other treatments, plus use of their exquisite oriental hammam and spa facilities, are available to all guests.

Food

The main L'Ortolan restaurant offers fresh Mediterranean dishes using local ingredients, many from the hotel's own garden. Ayurvedic or lighter spa meals can also be arranged by the chef and personalised to suit all needs and tastes. If you don't plan to go out and about, a half board option is useful as meals at the hotels' three restaurants can be quite pricey and add up on your final bill.

Fitness & Activities

The resort uses the natural beauty of the island to make your fitness fun and enjoyable. There are plenty of trails for jogging, and the island is particularly good for cycling. Yoga, Pilates and aqua-aerobic classes are all available in resort, plus there's tennis, squash, and a gym. We highly recommend taking a boat trip around the coast; it's the perfect way to witness Gozo's impressive coastal rock formations!

Location
Island of Gozo, Malta

Rooms
122

Freestyle Spa Facilities
Steam room, oriental hammam, and sauna in the spa, with an indoor heated swimming pool and whirlpool, alongside a relaxation area.

La Clairière

Deep in the lush forests of Alsace, La Clairière offers an eco-spa experience with incredible woodland surroundings. Through a combination of outdoor holistic treatments and organic food, their dedicated and nurturing team are on hand to help you re-root, grow, and re-energise.

Wellness Approach

A stay at pine-forested La Clairière brings you back to nature, providing the perfect place to re-connect with your inner self. Using treatments and techniques anchored around the five elements: fire, water, air, space and earth, La Clairière's experts utilise each of the five senses to promote deep relaxation, cleansing and deeper insight.

Food

La Clairière prides itself on providing an unforgettable organic culinary experience. Rise and shine each morning with an impressive, all-organic breakfast buffet including a spread of cereal, local cheese, bread and fruit, as well as the unique breakfast soup which is brimming with vitamins required to keep you alert and active throughout the day. Using only certified organic or wild ingredients to create a host of fresh vegetarian and fish dishes, La Clairière's in-house restaurant is perfect for those looking to lose weight, detox or relax deeply. The evening menu has a wide variety of organic dishes including tender lamb, seared scallops and colourful salads. For those not on a detox there's also an impressively elegant organic wine list.

Fitness & Activities

The enchanting location of La Clairière means that there are a number of outdoor activities to try. During the warm summer months you can enjoy outdoor yoga and qi gong classes, or take advantage of the forest walking and cycling trails. However those looking for an alternative energiser should try the oxygenation sessions, brave the ice fountain or tackle the climbing wall. There are also indoor activities including Pilates classes and a heated indoor swimming pool.

Location
La Petite Pierre, Alsace, France

Rooms
50

Freestyle Spa Facilities
Spa steam baths, saunas, whirlpools, indoor pool and a heated outdoor hydrotherapy pool.

Lefay Resort & Spa

Hidden away on a private estate high above Lake Garda and surrounded by lemon trees and olive groves, Lefay is a place where nature becomes nurture. From its state-of-the-art solar-panelled roof, exquisite natural products used in treatments and delicious, mainly organic food, this is a true eco-resort.

Wellness Approach

Fusing the principles of Traditional Chinese Medicine with western scientific research, Lefay's main aim is to recover your body's vital energy. All treatments use the Lefay SPA line of natural dermatological products, derived from precious medicinal plants. For relaxation you can't get much better than their huge spa, which is a veritable temple to wellness. Moving between the five unique saunas and pools feels like a ceremony of water and fire.

Food

The Lefay restaurants echo the resorts natural principles, and their gourmet food uses many local ingredients based on a Mediterranean diet rich in organic extra-virgin olive oil, citrus fruits and local herbs. Seasonal and of the highest quality, it is a healthy tribute to the Italian love of food. Don't worry – there is a special light menu for those trying to get back into shape...

Fitness & Activities

Within Lefay's extensive grounds there is a 2.5km running circuit, a fitness path with outdoor equipment, and a Chinese Medicine Energy path with therapeutic gardens rich in symbolism to remind us of the importance of contact with nature. Their fully equipped fitness centre, with state-of the art Technogym training equipment also encompasses an exercise studio for a choice of classes, including cardio fitness, postural gymnastics, body toning and Qi Gong. Then of course there is always the glorious lakeside to explore as well hiking, biking, golf and tennis.

Location
Lake Garda, Northern Italy

Rooms
90

Freestyle Spa Facilities
Lefay Spa is equipped with swimming pools, saunas and treatment areas, and extends into the surrounding park with areas for open-air activities.

SHA Wellness Clinic

To achieve optimum wellbeing, you need to balance how your body works, what you eat, drink, how you breathe and how you sleep. At this pioneering wellness clinic in Spain, you can learn to maximise your health, happiness and vitality with a mixture of natural therapies, holistic exercises and a Macrobiotic menu; the SHA diet.

Wellness Approach

SHA is an first-class pioneer of integrated wellness; taking the best from Oriental and Western medicine and combining them, along with an exceptional team of experts leading focused, goal-driven programmes. This is then supported by a modern Macrobiotic system of eating which is tailored to fit each individual's needs and is a therapy in itself. A major aspect is the zeal with which they teach, inspire and help you to aim for optimum health by making lifestyle-enhancing changes.

Food

Food at SHA is central to your stay and a key part of the wellness process, so every guest is served a personalised modern, healthy diet, so that you can access the healing power of nature through the finest organic foods. In very basic terms you won't see any coffee, tea, sugar, white flour or processed foods on the premises, and things like meat, chicken, eggs and dairy are recommended for occasional use only. The mainstay of a Macrobiotic diet is whole grains, vegetables, beans and pulses.

Fitness & Activities

The Life Learning Centre at SHA is a fantastic resource for those wanting to be active in their health and to learn how to make permanent changes and improvements to their wellbeing, be it through yoga, healthy cooking lessons, Tai Chi, Pilates, lectures in Macrobiotics and the yin & yang of food, as well as meditation. Don't miss their guided morning walks, often by the coast – a great way to meet other guests and kick-start your daily dose of wellbeing.

Location
Alicante, Spain

Rooms
93 Suites

Freestyle Spa Facilities
Aquarelax with underwater massage, resistance wall and jet stations around the pool, steam rooms, saunas, ice fountain, new heated swimming pool and Kneipp paths.

Shanti Maurice – A Nira Resort

A magical location between the dramatic mountains and white beaches of Southern Mauritius, the place instantly welcomes and cocoons. Add to that the sub-tropical climate, delicious food and warm welcoming staff and total relaxation ensues.

Wellness Approach

Based on Ayurvedic principles, the oldest medical tradition on earth, the spa concentrates on personalised programmes of treatments and therapies alongside yoga and meditation. All treatments and programmes are overseen by the resident Ayurvedic doctor and each visit begins with a full consultation after which a personal programme is prescribed – whether for weight loss, stress management or detoxification. Alongside the traditional Ayurvedic treatments is a wide choice of international therapies, water ceremonies, and Africology beauty rituals to choose from too.

Food

Individual diets or eating programmes are prescribed after the initial Ayurvedic consultation, according to each persons's body type or 'dosha', and unless you are on a weight loss programme, it's meant simply as a guide. That way each guest can learn a little about Ayurvedic principles but can also enjoy the resort's other dining options. The Fish and Rhum Shack, for instance, offers rustic beach side dining which highlights the best of Mauritian cuisine alongside delicious fusion dishes...not to mention the delights of the local distillery.

Fitness & Activities

Apart from the joys of the sea and the swimming pools, water sports and aqua aerobics are on offer along with a host of activities from nature walks to high tech cardio in the fully-equipped modern fitness centre. There are two outdoor floodlit tennis courts complete with tuition plus personal trainers for those who need them. Yoga and meditation classes take place daily, while private lessons can also be arranged too.

Location
St. Felix, South Coast
Mauritius

Rooms
61 suites & villas

Freestyle Spa Facilities
Sauna, steam room, Jacuzzi, large lap pool & heated Watsu seawater pool.

Spa Village Resort Tembok Bali

On the dramatic northeast coast of Bali, with its rugged mountains, volcanic black sand and emerald green lowlands, the adults-only Spa Village Resort Tembok, Bali is a place of peace and tranquillity where tired bodies and over-active minds can find respite and relaxation.

Wellness Approach

It is all about journeys... and your own particular journey to health, beauty and relaxation. There are three 'discovery paths' available, and you will find yours after your initial consultation with a therapist. It could be Balance, which is aimed at re-introducing equilibrium to body and mind and is ultra relaxing: or it might be Creativity, which releases all your own creative energies with the help and inspiration of Balinese arts: whilst Vigour will help you regain your strength, stamina and vitality through fitness. All paths include treatments and activities which take their strength from indigenous Balinese culture.

Food

Under a thatched roof and open to the sea and the drama of the slate-coloured sand, the Wantilan restaurant provides a feast for your eyes as well as your stomach. Organic, fresh and locally-sourced is the mantra of the restaurant with fruit, herbs and vegetables purchased from local farmers, while the seafood is straight from the ocean. Add to that the traditional tastes, sauces and spices of Balinese cuisine, for the most delicious of diets.

Fitness & Activities

If you enjoy diving or snorkelling, take a visit to the Tulamben wreck which is only a 30 minute drive away, where you can observe amazing marine life around the Liberty shipwreck or embark on one of the resort's cultural excursions and explore the creativity, history and traditions of this Island of the Gods.

We Love

Star-gazing meditation. A unique experience where you lie on a floating platform in the pool at night surrounded by candles, listening to meditative music and gazing at the stars. The feeling of weightlessness and the infinite night sky will calm busy and stress-filled minds.

Location
Tembok, Northeast Bali, Indonesia

Rooms
31

Freestyle Spa Facilities
Freestyle spa facilities are not available at this wellness resort.

SwaSwara

Set on a cliff top near to the legendary Om Beach, SwaSwara is a serene and secluded resort on the edge of temple town of Gokarna in Karwar, Karnataka – renowned as a pilgrimage site and a centre for Sanskrit learning. A land of paddy fields and coconut groves, and a much-loved home to yoga.

Wellness Approach

Yoga and Ayurveda are the key therapies at SwaSwara. Resident teachers offer at least five group yoga classes a day with different styles and different levels of experience, as well as Ayurveda treatments overseen by qualified Ayurvedic Doctors. This is enhanced by the chance to learn or practice meditation in the resort's beautiful blue meditation dome. Shaped as a mandala (a cosmic sphere depicting harmony), the dome has incredible acoustics ideal for accessing healing vibrations and aiding meditation.

Food

Apart from the delicious Ayurvedic cuisine of fresh fish and vegetables served every day, the resort is keen to teach you how to cook healthy food that compliments your doshas, or body type, so you can continue to eat healthily when you return home. However, if a breakfast curry is a bit too early for you, you can choose a continental breakfast option.

Fitness & Activities

On top of all that body conditioning yoga and meditation, why not explore your creative side with the resident art teacher, wander the Om beach, or learn how to make some truly tasty Indian dishes in their interactive open kitchen. Nearby spice markets are easy to visit by tuc-tuc. The high staff to guest ratio (90 staff for 24 rooms) means your stay will be personalised and you will be very well looked after, whatever you choose to do.

We Love

Laughter yoga. You may be sceptical at the start of this class with forced false laughter, but you will quickly find this turns to real giggles as it's quite infectious. Good for deepening the breath, toning the stomach and, best of all, lifting your spirits, as the natural mood enhancer of laughter increases the chemicals in your brain!

Location
Gokarna, Karnataka, India

Rooms
27 villas

Freestyle Spa Facilities
Freestyle spa facilities are not available at this very specialist wellness resort.

The BodyHoliday

Nestled on an idyllic Caribbean beach, The BodyHoliday is one of the friendliest resorts for a single traveller as well as sociable couples, as it's geared towards everyone having a happy, healthy time. The Activity Centre offers every type of water sport imaginable, while the included daily spa treatments are just heavenly.

Wellness Approach

Central to the resort's philosophy for a healthy holiday are the wellness pillars of relaxation, restorative beauty, exercise and a fresh, balanced diet. At the Oasis Spa, choose from invigorating scrubs, full body massages, purifying facials and hydrotherapy. Pampering, beauty and holistic treatments are carried out by first class complementary practitioners, while Ayurvedic therapies are available at the Ayurveda Pavilion.

Food

There are no rules about what you eat at The BodyHoliday, but you are given every opportunity to eat healthily, including advice from their highly qualified nutritional consultant, Michael Snader, who conducts workshops and is available for one-on-one consultations. There are four different restaurants, including Tao which is one of the world's sixty hot tables, plus if you're travelling alone, you can join a relaxed and sociable communal dining table.

Fitness & Activities

During your stay, you have the option to undergo a health and fitness analysis, carried out by a 'BodyGuard', one of the resort's specialists who can help you achieve your fitness and lifestyle goals while on holiday, plus also provide support on your return home. There's a comprehensive programme of sports and exercise with a full schedule of daily activities for a fun and adventurous stay. As well as water-based activities, there's a host of other activities to enjoy including tennis, archery, golf, Tai Chi and Pilates. Yoga is also exceptional at the resort, with a wide range of levels and styles.

We Love

Each holiday is all-inclusive, so from the food to the spa treatment to the activities, there's no need to worry about racking up extra expenses.

Location
St Lucia, Caribbean

Rooms
155

Freestyle Spa Facilities
Main pool, relaxation pool, sports pool and whirlpool.

Ti Sana

Charming yet contemporary, Ti Sana was created around a former merchant's home in the heart of a sleepy hamlet in rural northern Italy. Ti Sana means 'to take care of yourself', which is apt as the peaceful setting and expert team create an intimate and nurturing experience.

Wellness Approach

Offering a complete holistic approach to wellness, every programme contains a balance of spa treatments, gentle physical activity and clean nutrition to allow you to re-connect. Ti Sana only uses certified organic, biological body products, to match their philosophy of being in harmony with nature. By nourishing your body with fresh mainly raw foods and mineral-rich juices, you're completely supported during a detox cleanse or weight-management programme. The results speak for themselves; bright eyes, a beaming complexion and increased energy.

Food

Ti Sana has an exclusively plant based philosophy. Their head chef is a vegetarian, raw food nutritional specialist, crafting menus designed to cleanse, purify and energise the body. The juice fast includes organic raw fruits and vegetables, whilst the raw and warmed food menu nourishes the body with pure, fresh ingredients such as sunflower seeds, soy sprouts and sea vegetables. The overall aim is long-lasting; to re-educate and re-set your lifestyle to ensure you're able to make positive changes once you're at home.

Fitness & Activities

Activities at Ti Sana centre around Traditional Chinese Medicine, such as Tai Chi, Qigong and Lian Gong, plus morning riverside power walks and yoga. A complimentary optional group excursion takes place each week, such as a lesson in healthy food shopping, a visit to a designer shopping outlet or a transfer to beautiful Lake Como. Add to that educational daily staff tips and talks from visiting health experts, with time to unwind, and you may never want to leave.

Location
Lombardy, North Italy

Rooms
22

Freestyle Spa Facilities
A circuit of saunas, aromatic showers, a small chromotherapy pool plus fresh and salted hydrotherapies.

glossary

Abhyanga
A full Ayurvedic body massage, using specific herbal oils according to your body type, followed by a steam bath and hot shower.

Acupressure Massage
A Chinese massage which manipulates the body's pressure points to release blocked energies and to stimulate the flow of energy through the body.

Acupuncture
Part of Traditional Chinese Medicine, it employs the body's own energy to help heal itself. Using the same points as in acupressure, tiny, fine needles are used to increase the flow of energy in the body.

Affusion Shower
Hydro-massage consisting of a fine mist of warm seawater applied to the whole body by means of a horizontal shower.

Algae Body Wrap
A warm seaweed wrap that relieves muscular and joint aches, pains and strains. Helps relieve skin conditions.

Aromatherapy
Treatments such as massage, facials, body wraps, or hydrobaths that include the application of fragrant essential oils. Different oils are used for different therapeutic benefits.

Ayurveda
One of the oldest medical disciplines in the world. Founded in India and now stretching worldwide, it incorporates a variety of techniques from meditation to massage, and from diet to herbal medicines. The word in Sanskrit means 'Science of Life' and it is geared to rebalance the body.

Ayurvedic Consultation
All Ayurvedic programmes begin with a detailed consultation with a doctor who will then determine your 'dosha' and proscribe a specific programme for you.

Balinese Massage
Using traditional Javanese massage oils and techniques, this is a strong massage which incorporates rolling and long kneading strokes.

Balneotherapy
The use of underwater massage to stimulate, massage and relieve tension in the body.

Blitz Massage or Shower
A water jet massage or shower, which helps decongest fatty deposits and relaxes tense muscles.

Body Peeling
Gently removes dead skin cells and leaves the skin supple and silky-smooth. Prepares the skin for increased absorption of products.

Breathwork
Breathwork is the use of Breath Awareness and Conscious Breathing (exercises and techniques), as a tool for health in spirit, mind and body. Every psychological, emotional, chemical and physiological state has an associated breathing pattern. As you change from one state to another, your breathing pattern changes, and vice versa. If you experiment with your breath, you can trigger different thinking and states of being.

Chi Nei Tsang
A classical Taoist abdominal massage originating from Traditional Chinese Medicine, which is usually part of a comprehensive detox programme.

Chinese Tuina Massage

Tuina is an important part of Traditional Chinese Medicine (TCM). Tuina uses techniques and manipulations to stimulate acupuncture points or other parts of the body surface to correct physical, as well as physiological, imbalances within the body.

Classical Massage

Relaxes and loosens stiff muscles.

Colonic Hydrotherapy

An intense water irrigation of the entire colon, intended to cleanse trapped impurities, preventing the recycling of toxins into the bloodstream.

Cortisol

Cortisol is a steroid hormone made in the adrenal glands which is released in response to stress and a low level of blood glucocorticoid. Its primary functions are to increase blood sugar through gluconeogenesis, suppress the immune system, and aid the metabolism of fat, protein, and carbohydrate. It also decreases bone formation.

Deep Tissue Massage

A restorative massage that aids in releasing deep held patterns of tension, removing toxins, relaxing, soothing and encouraging muscles to operate at full capacity.

Detox

A programme of treatments and nutrition to help the body rid itself of toxins.

Dosha

The 3 main doshas used in Ayurvedic Medicine (sometimes translated into English as humours) are: Vata (combination of the space and air elements), Pitta (analogous to the fire element), and Kapha (combination of water and earth elements).

Discover & Unwind™

Our Discover & Unwind™ range combines visits to special sightseeing locations with spa treatments onsite so you enjoy exploration as well as relaxation. Boat trips, food tasting, picnics at scenic spots and guided walking tours, are examples of some of the activities on the menu plus of course some proper pampering back in resort. Ideal for both single travellers and our couples wanting to venture off the property.

Dry Brush Massage

This massage uses stroking techniques applied in a special way with a brush of half bristles. It helps increase blood circulation in the skin and removes the dead skin cells from the upper skin layer, making the skin surface smoother and more receptive in preparation for certain nourishing skin packs. It is suitable for detoxification and cellulite treatments owing to its effect as a metabolism stimulator.

Fango

The Italian word for mud. Used in treatments as a heat pack, to help detoxify the body, smooth the skin, stimulate circulation and soothe tired or aching muscles.

Fitness Training

A complete fitness and exercise programme with a fitness expert. This customised approach will compliment all other therapies and activities that you experience during your stay.

Flexible Fitness™

We developed our exclusive FlexFit™ programmes to allow you the flexibility to choose exactly the kind of personalised exercise plan that suits you. With five privately coached fitness sessions in every programme alongside a plethora of facilities and group activities, you can now work on your fitness with inspiring activities enhanced by expert guidance in stunning surroundings.

Floatation Bed

Relax while floating within a water bed. It has the most relaxing womb-like effect, as the water takes the full weight of the body.

Foot Acupressure

Massage applied to the zones of your feet that correspond to all the parts of the body and internal organs. The treatment stimulates the body's own healing and balancing process.

Gommage

A cleansing, rehydrating treatment using creams and lotions, which are applied in massage-type movements.

Hammam

A Turkish or middle-Eastern bathing area which uses steam, water and oils.

Hopi Candle

A Hopi candle, made of flax, honey and herbs, is gently inserted into the outer ear to treat sinusitis, rhinitis, earwax, earache and tinnitus.

Hot Stone Massage

Smooth volcanic or basalt stones have been used for centuries by different cultures to increase the pressure of a massage, thus helping its efficacy in relieving tension.

Hydrotherapy

Treatments using water either in underwater massage, jet blitzes, showers or mineral baths.

Kneipp

Thermal treatments created by Father Sebastian Kneipp which use a mixture of hot and cold water, as well as a number of herbal essences, mostly to help increase circulation.

Lymphatic Drainage

A therapy in which the practitioner uses a range of specialised and gentle rhythmic pumping techniques to move the skin in the direction of the lymph flow. This stimulates the lymphatic vessels, which carry substances vital to the defence of the body and remove waste products.

Marma Massage

An energising massage of the marma points (specific energy centres). This revitalising massage stimulates the circulatory, immune and nervous systems, and also helps to restore energy.

Mineral or Thermal Bath

Special baths in areas where spring waters are naturally infused with minerals. Depending on the minerals, such therapies help with muscle relaxation, rheumatic and bronchial problems.

Moxibustion

A Chinese therapeutic technique, which involves the application of heat to areas of skin near acupuncture points or energy pathways, to help boost the result of a treatment or massage.

Mud Pack

The packs are directly applied to the skin and are beneficial in the treatment of rheumatic complaints and muscular problems. The mud can be used for either full or partial packs, depending on the doctor's prescription. The pack temperature is normally 40°C. The effect of the hot mud helps regulate circulation.

Naturopathy

The roots of naturopathy are found in the ancient Greece of Hippocrates, who recognised and wrote about the healing power of nature. As a specific discipline, naturopathy is related to the traditional European nature cure, which uses dietary, nutrition and detoxification techniques alongside physiotherapy, herbal medicine and acupuncture.

pH Balance

pH stands for power of hydrogen, which is a measurement of the hydrogen ion concentration in the body. pH is used to measure how acid or alkaline your blood is. Maintaining a proper ratio between acid and alkaline foods in our diet are vital for our health. The proper pH level in the human blood and tissues should be approximately 7.365, which is slightly alkaline. You can test your pH balance by checking your saliva or urine, using pH strips.

Phytotherapy

Medicinal plants have been used since the dawn of time. Man has in fact always searched for plants that were able to treat symptoms, syndromes and more generally, the different disorders he inevitably suffered. Plant extracts delivered in the form of herbal teas, are offered for their medicinal properties. Each medicinal plant is made up of a precise 'personality' that integrates with the human constitution.

Qi Gong

A Chinese system of prescribed physical exercises or movements, performed in a meditative state.

Reflexology

An ancient Chinese technique that uses pressure-point massage (usually on the feet, but also on the hands and ears) to restore the flow of energy throughout the entire body.

Reiki

A holistic and natural energy healing system, Reiki practitioners channel energy to restore the body's energy field to its natural frequency, which can bring about deep relaxation, remove energy blockages, detoxify the body and provide healing.

Relaxing Massage

This massage concentrates on soothing away tiredness, stress and alleviating tension, inducing relaxation to the body and mind.

Scalp Massage

This heavenly massage will awaken your brain, stimulate hair growth and relax your entire body.

Shiatsu

Japanese form of massage which involves a powerful stimulation of the body's pressure points to invigorate and relax. Combined with stretching, palming and mobilising movements, this massage also loosens profound muscular tension.

Shirodhara

Warm oil is poured on the forehead continuously, followed by an Ayurvedic face, neck, head, shoulder, hand and foot massage, using specific organic oils, to relieve mental stress and restore calm.

Sports Massage

Especially beneficial if you are suffering from aches, pains and stiffness. The masseur will help to relieve tension from specific areas of your body, improving circulation and mobility.

Tai Chi

A Chinese martial art of stylized gestures regulated by deep breathing and movement.

Thai Massage

One of the few massages where oil is not used, instead it is performed over light cotton pyjamas. A manipulation of the body using yoga-like stretching, pummelling and kneading, as well as the exertion of pressure along the body's energy channels, to help release blockages and soothe tight limbs and muscles.

Therapeutic Massage

A full-body massage to ease tense muscles and soothe away aches and pains.

Tibetan Massage

Tibetan massage focuses on lymphatic drainage, acupressure and meridian work, using hot Himalayan salt poultices, infused herbs and spices to help stimulate energy flow.

Traditional Chinese Medicine

A broad range of medicine practices developed in China for over 2000 years. Doctors access the body's condition through examining the eyes, tongue, and skin pallor, in order to understand the physical and emotional story of the body. They then prescribe treatments that de-stress and rejuvenate.

Vedanta

The essential philosophy original to the Hindus which typically complements Ayurveda.

Watsu

A form of body massage performed whilst lying in warm water, where a therapist stretches and moves the body against the flow of water. A womb-like experience and truly relaxing.

Wellbeing Boosters™

A range of programmes designed by Wellbeing Escapes. Wellbeing Boosters™ are a lighter wellbeing range that mix relaxing and therapeutic spa treatments, with nutritious food and energising activities. Ideal if you're short of time, are trying a wellbeing break for the first time, or just want to be pampered and feel good.

Picture Credits

Wellbeing Escapes would like to thank the following resorts for permission to reproduce their material on the following pages:

Front Cover (Clockwise from Top Left): 'Walking on Beach' – iStockphoto, 'Healthy Woman and Man Doing Yoga' – iStockphoto, 'Herbs' – *Six Senses, Balancing Senses Collection*, 'Portrait of a Young Woman in a Natural Pool' – iStockphoto

01. 'Hammock Relaxation' – iStockphoto

02. 'Happy Young Woman Drinking Coconut Milk on Beach' – iStockphoto

04. 'Breakfast Anytime' – *Fusion Maia*

06. 'Beach Yoga' – iStockphoto

08–09. 'Infinity Pool' – *Porto Elounda*

11. Top to Bottom: 'Only the Freshest Ingredients for this Chef' and 'Tightening Those Tummys – Yoga' – iStockphoto

12–13. 'Qi Gong' – *Six Senses*

14. 'Fitness with a View' – iStockphoto

15. 'Chinese Herbs' – iStockphoto

16. 'Guest Experience' – *Kamalaya Wellness Sanctuary*

17. 'Segara Girl' – *Spa Village Tembok Bali*

18. 'Stress Busting Smoothie' – Saskia Gregson-Williams at hipandhealthy.com

19. 'Thinking Alone' – iStockphoto

20. 'White Lotus' – Shutterstock

21. 'Yoga 04' – *Fusion Maia*

22. Top to Bottom: 'Hands Playing with Fresh Water' and 'Girl on a Bridge' – iStockphoto

23. 'All Are One' – iStockphoto

25. 'Beautiful Young Woman in White Sportswear Running on Beach' – Shutterstock

26. 'Digital Stopwatch' – iStockphoto

27. 'Biking' – *Kempinski San Lawrenz*

28. 'Beach Warm Up' – iStockphoto

30. 'Tai Chi' – *COMO Shambhala Estate*

32. 'Gluten Free Power-up Pancakes' – Saskia Gregson-Williams at naturallysassy.co.uk

33. 'Boy Jumping' – iStockphoto

34. 'Tape Measure' – Shutterstock

35. 'Athletic Runner Celebrates Achieving Her Fitness Goals' – iStockphoto

36. 'Young Woman in Bathtub Using Body Brush on Leg' – Shutterstock

37. 'Peeled Orange' – iStockphoto

38. 'Miso Soup' – iStockphoto

39. 'Steam Room' – iStockphoto

40. 'Lemons' – Shutterstock

41. 'Berries' – iStockphoto

42. Top to Bottom: 'Life's Enjoyment' – iStockphoto and 'Herbs' – *Six Senses, Balancing Senses Collection*

43. 'Floating' – *COMO Shambhala Estate*

44. 'Marinara Zucchini Fettucini' – *Absolute Sanctuary*

45. 'We Always Feel Great After a Surf' – iStockphoto

46. 'Mortar and Pestle with Spices' – iStockphoto

47. 'Essential Oil for Aromatherapy' – iStockphoto

48. 'Smiling Woman Sitting in Kitchen with an Orange Juice' – iStockphoto

49. 'Honey in Jar with Honey Dipper on Vintage Wooden Background' – Shutterstock

51. 'Garden Salad' – *Kamalaya Wellness Sanctuary*

52. 'Drinking Water' – iStockphoto

53. 'Woman on Vacation in the Caribbean' – iStockphoto

54. 'Inspired Women Lies' – iStockphoto

56–57. 'Breakfast Anytime 3' – *Fusion Maia*

88. 'Man – Recreation, Rest, Relaxation and Massage' – iStockphoto

95. 'Walking on Beach' – iStockphoto

Acknowledgments

Wellbeing Escapes would like to thank the following for generously sharing their knowledge, expertise and time:

Doctor Andy Jones at Nuffield Health

Stuart Bold at The Meditation Foundation

Graeme Marsh our fitness instructor

Ian Marber at ianmarber.com

Elizabeth Montgomery at holisticnutrition.co.uk

Doctor Simone Laubscher at Rejuv, Harley Street

Saskia Gregson-Williams at naturallysassy.co.uk and hipandhealthy.com

And a big thanks to our wonderful and hardworking interns Louise Jones and Sam Byers for all their research and writing too.